SPE

Bude and Stratton
in old picture postcards

by Rennie Bere and Roy Thorn

European Library ZALTBOMMEL / THE NETHERLANDS

GB ISBN 90 288 3094 4

© 1985 European Library – Zaltbommel/The Netherlands

Third edition, 1997: reprint of the original edition of 1985.

INTRODUCTION

In 1880 Bude was a busy little port with the coastal trade in full flow. Small sailing ships, mostly ketches, brought coal, limestone and trade goods into the harbour and through the great sea-lock. Corn and bark for tanning were the main exports. The canal trade was less extensive than it had been a decade earlier as the railway had already reached Holsworthy. Even so, immediate land links still depended upon horses, coaches and your own flat feet. Summer visitors came in small numbers.

By 1930 the coastal trade had almost ended, and few ships used the harbour. The canal was closed (except to rowing-boats) above the lower wharfs. The main link with the rest of the world was the railway. Tourism was growing steadily. Most of the major hotels looked much as they do today. There was little fishing and few signs of industry but the banks and many of the shops we now use were well established. Today seafishing – though mainly a leisure pursuit – is a popular activity; and there is a growing industrial estate. But the main emphasis is on tourism, controlled by sound planning so that it does not despoil the environment.

Bude itself is a relative newcomer. At the beginning of the last century it was little more than an outlying part of the parish of Stratton where sailing ships could be beached upon the strand and the River Neet crossed at low tide. There were an ancient manor house and a few other buildings but nothing to suggest what has now evolved. The town is essentially a Victorian development built up on the port and canal trade.

Stratton was, and indeed still is, an ancient market town clustering round its fine old church – very much an entity in its own right. Poughill, where there is another fine church, was a small village and a separate manor now absorbed into the Bude-Stratton complex. Marhamchurch is just outside the modern boundaries. Morwenstow, Kilkhampton and Week St. Mary, which once had the status of a borough, are near but quite independent.

Until late in the 18th century, the two principal landowning families were the Arundells of Trerice and the Grenvilles of Stowe (between Bude and Morwenstow), Kilkhampton and Bideford. Their lands met in what is now the town of Bude and were connected by the ford which crossed the River Neet at Efford – the name derives from 'ebbing ford'. And, so far as our area is concerned, the outstanding member of the distinguished Grenville family was the Civil War hero, Sir Bevil, who fought and won the battle of Stamford Hill (at Stratton) for the royalist cause in 1643. The family of Thynne eventually inherited the Grenville lands while those of Arundell devolved upon Sir Thomas Acland, these two families dominating the development of Bude throughout the Victorian period and until the Second World War. Sir Thomas Acland, in particular, was closely concerned with the harbour and canal undertakings, the lower reaches of the canal passing through his land.

Little now remains of the canal beyond the two mile stretch along the flat, wide alluvial valley which leads inland from the lock-gates. The canal was supplied with water from the reservoir now known as Lower Tamar Lake, near Kilkhampton, and originally served Holsworthy, Launceston and numerous intermediate stations. Its main purpose was to distribute coal from the harbour and carry the lime-rich sea-sand, produced by erosion of the cliffs and the breakdown of shells, to farms in the hinterland where it had been used as a manure from times immemorial; produce was also exported. The line of the canal passed through hilly country – there was no alternative – far too steep for conventional locks, though there were plenty of these. The answer was found in a series of 'inclined planes', the longest of which (just above Marhamchurch) was 225 feet (68 metres) in vertical height and 935 feet (285 metres) long where a 'well and bucket' method was used. Two wells were sunk from the top of the plane to the level of its bottom. A huge bucket, with a capacity of 15 tons of water, was suspended in each well and connected by chains over a drum-wheel. The descending bucket provided the power to raise a wheeled tub-boat carrying a five ton load. When the bucket reached the bottom, a valve opened and the water escaped. Other shorter planes were powered by water-wheels. The Bude canal was, for its period, a remarkable feat of engineering – the longest tub-boat canal in Britain – all too soon to be made obsolete by the railway age.

Stratton, Kilkhampton and Week St. Mary are believed to have evolved from Bronze Age settlements alongside an ancient ridgeway. This was the natural line of communication by land, the same general route being followed by the modern A39 trunk road which connects Bude with north Devon in one direction and with the heart of Cornwall in the other. By contrast, Bude Haven (the postal address until after the 1930s) was the only break in the long line of cliffs, stretching from Hartland Point to the Camel estuary, which offered any real protection for sailing ships during rough weather and which provided reasonably safe beaching – an obvious place for a small harbour. Even so, the high stark cliffs and the countless rocky ribs jutting into the sea made it an extremely hazardous haven, particularly in winter as some of the pictures in this collection will show.

It is these cliffs, the wild seas below and the sense of isolation which provide the neighbourhood with its greatest attraction: the riches of the natural environment. The slate and sandstone cliffs are exposed to the full force of the Atlantic and the battering of waves and weather. The rocks and cliff strata are folded into fantastic shapes and zigzag patterns; some rock nodules enclose the remains of a fossilized fish unique to the area. The rock pools, revealed by the passage of the tides, support many different forms of seashore life. Wherever a break in the cliffs allows plants to take root, they are swathed in glorious wild flowers. Among them, rock samphire grows close to the sea and bands of thrift border the cliff-edge in summer with many colourful grassland flowers.

There is equal interest in the birds: seabirds and waders with smaller species in the furze. The canal, the marshes beside it and the little estuary of the River Neet attract plovers, curlew and migrating wild-fowl. Usually there are herons, and a kingfisher sometimes perches on a wharfing post in the harbour. Grey Atlantic seals occasionally visit the bay from breeding caves further down the coast. The recently extinct large blue butterfly had one of its last British haunts near Bude. To accommodate some of this wildlife two nature reserves have been established actually in the town: the district council's Canal Marshes Reserve, where reed-beds and pools are overlooked by a hide, and Phillips's Point on the way to Widemouth where access is unrestricted and coastal flowers are plentiful. The best of the cliff lands are permanently protected; and Tamar Lake, constructed to provide water for the canal, is a splendid refuge for wintering wildfowl.

We have aimed in this collection to depict as many aspects as possible of the past life of the place but are conscious of certain gaps, some of which are covered by this introduction. Though many of the pictures come from our own albums we have sought help from several friends and from Bude-Stratton Town Council's Historical and Folk Exhibition. We gratefully acknowledge this help and would particularly mention Andrew Jewell, Bryan Dudley Stamp, Brendon Parsons, Michael Johns, Michael Smith, Beatrice Barker and Peter Cloke who, as harbourmaster, upholds a splendid tradition.

1. It is not easy, even with modern equipment, to capture the movement of the waves with a camera. Yet this beautiful picture was taken by Thorn of Bude in the early years of this century – an outstanding photograph for the period – and soon became a popular postcard. It shows the Atlantic rollers breaking on the rocks outside the breakwater and explains better than words can do why the haven was such a difficult harbour to enter under unassisted sail and why Bude beaches have become such excellent centres of modern surfing. *Break, break, break/ On thy cold gray stones, O Sea!/ And I would that my tongue could utter/ The thoughts that arise in me.* (Alfred Tennyson.)

BUDE BREAKWATER & WHALE BACK ROCK 127

2. Bude breakwater protects the harbour. The original structure, begun in 1819, had high steep sides and an imposing pier-head but was destroyed by a storm in 1838. The present breakwater was then built and has survived the gales of the last 150 years with surprisingly little damage. It is less pretentious than its predecessor but more effective, standing only four feet above the level of a high spring tide, the gentle slope of its seaward face offering little resistance to the waves. It is a pleasant walk at any time, but when the sea is running high it has been a popular and spectacular viewing point throughout its history. This photograph was taken about 1910.

3. Sir Thomas' Pit, at the end of the breakwater, was Bude's first bathing pool. Constructed by blocking off the seaward end of a natural channel between two ribs of rock, it was and still is filled by the tides. At first used largely by Sir Thomas Acland's family and friends, it was opened to the public – 'with graduated depth for gentlemen' but certainly not ladies – during the second half of the last century when a small charge was raised. It remained Bude's only bathing pool until the early 1930s when the large Summerleaze Beach pool was constructed. The Pit is still popular, particularly with children, many of whom have learned to swim there.

4. A familiar scene in old Bude with sailing ships in the canal — a smack, a ketch and a schooner — ready to pass out through the lock-gates when the tide is high enough; others wait under the lee of the breakwater. Chapel Rock, which was actually cut by the breakwater, stands out particularly well in this photograph taken about 1903. Chapel Rock was the site of a mediaeval chapel and was occupied by a hermit, holy man or 'bede' whose duty it was to keep a fire burning to guide ships into the haven. The origin of the name Bude is uncertain but is thought to derive from this chapel and its occupant, the haven being known to sailors as 'Haven of the Holy Man' or 'Bede's Haven' as it often appears on early maps.

10192. COMPASS POINT. BUDE. —JUDGES' LTD

5. Compass Point, which guards the southern approach to the haven, is one of the finest natural features on the coast. The photograph was taken about 1900, and a casual glance suggests little change since then. But if you compare the picture with the scene today, you will notice changes in detail brought about by erosion which is going on all the time. The great prow of hard sandstone remains. The Storm Tower or 'Temple of the Winds' was built by Sir Thomas Acland in the 1820s; a necessary shelter for observing the movement of ships, it was used as a Coastguard Station until the new station was built on Efford Beacon. Shortly after this photograph was taken, the tower had to be dismantled and rebuilt a few yards further back from the cliff edge.

CANAL AND BEACH FROM MENTONE VIEW
BOARDING HOUSE. BUDE.

6. In this picture, taken about 1925, a single ketch is seen in the canal just after passing through the lock-gates. Across the canal, a man is towing the ship along by means of a hawser, while she is accompanied by a throng of excited holiday-makers – there is always a thrill about even the smallest ship entering port. There are a few bathing huts on the beach beyond but, since this photograph was taken, most of the sand-dunes have been removed to make room for more huts and so deprive the higher levels of the beach of their natural defences. To its credit the Local Authority is now attempting to reclaim the small area of dunes that still remains.

New Swing Bridge over the Canal Bude   Thorn photo

7. About 500 yards above the sea-lock, where the canal is now crossed by a main road, there used to be a swing-bridge which allowed ships to pass into the upper basin (see no. 9). This picture, from 1906, shows the new swing-bridge, which had replaced an earlier wooden structure, shortly after its installation; the beginning of the tow-path can also be seen. The Falcon Hotel, a landmark since the early 19th century, and some of the Falcon Terrace cottages are visible beyond the bridge with St. Michael's church nearby. Some of these cottages, almost unchanged in outward appearance, have become the Brendon Arms, unofficial centre of seafaring Bude.

8. This photograph shows the work of the port in progress with three ships alongside lower wharf. Two have not been identified but furthest from the camera is *Kindly Light,* a steel-hulled ketch adorned by the figurehead of an angel with book which, however, did not protect her from being sunk by a German submarine in the First World War. In the background are the low buildings of Bude's Primary School. Established during the 19th century as a Church of England school, it has retained links with the church. Among the many teachers who have helped to give Bude children a good start in life one name stands out: James Arthur, schoolmaster from 1861 to 1905. There were schools in Stratton and some of the villages long before Bude.

9. The upper basin of the canal with Petherick's wharehouses as they appeared in 1924 with several lorries and a single horse-drawn coal-cart, symbolizing the beginning of one era and the end of another. These buildings have changed little externally but instead of advertising wool, coal and grain they now proclaim 'Adventure Days' and serve as a centre for adventure training and holidays: canoeing, surfing, rock climbing and many other vigorous activities. Immediately to the left of this picture was Stapleton's shipyard, established in 1830 and worked by the same family until about 1916. Ships, which always had to be launched and taken out of the water sideways, were built, altered and repaired; the last big job was the conversion of the ketch *Lady Acland* into *Agnes* which was finally wrecked in the Caribbean in 1955.

On the Canal, Bude.

10. When the railway reached Bude the canal, as opposed to the harbour, ceased to be used commercially. Below the first lock, it then became popular for rowing boats, canoes and coarse fishing. This still is the situation during the summer months when Bruce Sampson finds numerous customers for his boats. This picture was taken in the 1920s but, except for the trees, might have been taken today. The decline in the number of trees along and near the verges of the canal is a sad fact of life. It is not all the fault of man as, during recent years, disease has killed many fine elms. Some clumps of willows have been planted but much more needs to be done to return the canal to its former beauty.

11. This photograph of Breakwater Road, which runs alongside the canal between Falcon Bridge (former swing-bridge) and the sea-lock, was taken about 1910 when shipping was still plentiful. The cottages on the left, originally known as Canal Terrace cottages, were built in the 1830s for canal workers. Soon, many of them were taken over by sea-captains and named after the ships they sailed. Some of these names survive – *Jessamine* and *Hazel,* for example – and many of the cottages retain a great deal of their old world charm. The first four cottages at the landward end were converted into a boarding house in the 1920s but this did not survive. Alterations elsewhere have been in keeping with the surroundings.

12. The canal and swing-bridge are here seen from the tow-path, a short distance above the bridge. Major alterations to the Falcon Hotel had been completed and it looks much as it does today except for the design and shape of the cars. There is a ketch in the lower wharf; and if you look through the bars of the bridge you can see the Old Forge where horses were shoed which towed barges up the canal and brought sand from the beach — the Old Forge is now a small museum, Bude Folk and Historical Exhibition. This photograph was probably taken in 1923 just before the swing-bridge was replaced by a permanent structure which made the upper canal finally inaccessible to shipping.

13. This photograph, probably taken in 1905, shows Captain Frederick Martin, of Bude, being presented with a clock and barometer by two Boscastle fishermen whom he rescued after they had been blown out to sea in a storm. Captain Martin also knew what it meant to be rescued. He was master of *Hawk,* an elegant little ketch, when she was wrecked below Maer Cliff in August 1897 when leaving Bude with a load of scrap-iron destined for Swansea; and of *President Garfield* which came to grief while entering the haven in March 1906. The last named was launched as a schooner in 1881 but later changed to ketch rigging better suited to this coast.

Ceres of Bude Built 1811.

20. Petherick Photo

14. *Ceres* is seen rounding Barrel Rock at the end of the breakwater, always a tricky manoeuvre for a sailing ship when a heavy sea was running. *Ceres,* the best loved of all Bude ketches, was built at Salcombe in Devon in 1811 and saw service on the coast of Spain during the Peninsular War. She came to Bude in 1826 and was bought by Henry Petherick in 1852. She remained with this well-known Bude family for four generations and traded in and out of the haven until 1936 when she sprang a leak and sank in the Bristol Channel, her crew being rescued by the Appledore lifeboat. She had been for many years the oldest ship on the British register. No member of her many crews was ever lost at sea.

15. This photograph of *Ceres* under full sail was taken in 1912 and shows her entering the calm water under the lee of the breakwater. She carries the typical rig of a ketch, the final development of British wooden merchant sailing vessels – 'the last development of the wooden sailing ships which had been one of western man's principal tools in gaining ascendancy over most of the rest of the world,' according to W.J. Slade and Basil Greenhill in *West Country Coasting Ketches* (Conway Maritime Press, 1974). *Ceres* is being met by the hobblers in their open rowing boat. It was rare for a ship under sail to enter the haven without them. They acted as pilot and took ropes from the vessel, making them fast to posts along the channel. It was a vital service.

16. This picture of *Ceres,* taken on a calm summer day in 1920, shows her rounding the breakwater under the power of her own engine. When she first came to Bude, *Ceres* was a single masted smack. She was lengthened in Stapleton's yard in 1868 and given the full ketch rigging; the auxiliary engine was fitted in 1912. This not only facilitated entry into port, it enabled her to stay close inshore during the First World War when enemy submarines threatened. *Ceres* was not only a local coaster. She sailed regularly to London, Liverpool, Ireland and various North Sea ports, even when over a hundred years old. She had many close calls during her long life but survived.

17. Two schooners in the harbour together were an uncommon sight as few were short enough to pass through the lock-gates. Schooners, moreover, were less easy to manoeuvre than ketches near this rocky coast. The ships in this photograph, taken about 1880, have not been identified with certainty but are thought to be *Annie Davey,* a Bude vessel, and *Crystal Spring* (see no. 21). An earlier Bude schooner, *Elizabeth Scown,* with Captain Sluggett as master, was wrecked on the rocks of the breakwater in 1877 when carrying stone for enlargement of St. Michael's Church. The lifeboat capsized when attempting a rescue and her coxswain, James Maynard, was drowned. He was the only casualty and the only man not wearing the regulation cork jacket of the period.

18. This photograph, taken in the late 1880s, shows the crew of *Ant* with her master, Captain Hines. This ketch, originally built as a smack, had an adventurous life. She first struck the breakwater in 1868 and was finally sunk off Trevose Head after colliding with a Padstow schooner in July 1897. Her most alarming misadventure occurred during the blizzard of 1891 (see no. 44) when she was bringing coal from Pembrokeshire to Bude. Blown right off course and hopelessly disabled, she was sighted by a clipper more than 200 miles beyond the Isles of Scilly. The cabin boy had died of exposure. Master and mate were exhausted, frost-bitten and huddled in the folds of a sail. They were transferred to the clipper, and *Ant* was sailed to Plymouth.

19. The disasters described with the last picture were not the only ones suffered by *Ant*, and she is seen here in 1890 shortly before being stranded on the Bude sands – this happened to her four times. Two years earlier *Alford* and *Elizabeth*, both Bude ketches, had been stranded together on Summerleaze Beach. *Alford* was finally lost off the Netherlands. *Elizabeth*, built at Salcombe in 1838, was eventually wrecked on the Summerleaze cliffs in 1912 while bringing coal from Wales. Today her mast stands on Summerleaze Down as a flagstaff which is dressed overall on special occasions.

20. The first steamer to be wrecked or stranded at Bude was the small Cardiff collier, *Llandaff,* which was driven on to the breakwater in 1899. She had a remarkable escape for she ended up with her bow in the air above the end of Sir Thomas' Pit in which she left most of her cargo — surreptitiously collected by local residents. She was refloated from this strange situation and returned to Cardiff. Several other steamers came to grief during the early decades of this century, one of the worst spots being Northcott Mouth, about a mile north of the haven: the London collier *Woodbridge* in 1915, her crew of thirty-three being rescued by breeches-buoy; *Belem* from Gibraltar in 1917 and the Falmouth tug *Arwenack* in 1920.

21. The schooner *Crystal Spring* (see no. 17) traded regularly with Bude. In August 1904, while bringing a cargo into the haven in a northerly gale, she was driven on to the rocks below Summerleaze Down. As she was breaking up her master, Captain Malloy, and mate were rescued by the rocket and breeches-buoy apparatus in the presence of a large crowd of visitors and residents. Four years earlier, two even larger sailing ships had been wrecked: the Neapolitan barque *Concezione,* carrying pit-props to Swansea, was battered to pieces on the Widemouth rocks; and the Austrian barque, *Capricorno,* carrying coal from Cardiff to the Adriatic, was driven on to the rocks near the breakwater. Only two of her crew of fourteen were saved.

22. This photograph of the Lifeboat House, just above Falcon Bridge, was taken about 1890 and shows the crew outside the building which was presented to the Royal National Lifeboat Institution in 1865 in memory of Elizabeth Moore Garden, wife of Robert Theolophilus Garden, by their surviving children — the land was given by Sir Thomas Acland. It remained in use until 1924 when the lifeboat was withdrawn from Bude. For some years the building was unused. It then became a store for a local transport company and inevitably something of an eyesore. It has subsequently been converted, with a minimum of external alteration, for human occupation, its origins being remembered by the carved inscription above the entrance.

23. The Garden family, which had no direct connection with Bude, not only gave the town its Lifeboat House but provided three successive boats. Appropriately these were named *Elizabeth Moore Garden I, II* and *III,* the last two being launched in 1886 and 1911 respectively. This photograph shows the third of these boats being launched into the canal soon after her arrival at the haven. Harry Barrett, the coxswain, is at the helm. A good crowd of residents and visitors, in their panama hats and 'straw boaters', admire his skill.

24. This unusual photograph shows *Elizabeth Moore Garden II* entering the sea-lock in the summer of 1904. We do not know the occasion but the calm sea and relaxed crowd suggest an exercise rather than a genuine rescue, though the picture was taken about the time of the *Crystal Spring* disaster. The canal did not prove a satisfactory means of getting the lifeboat out to sea or back again. Passage through the lock depends entirely on the state of the tides — only when the tide is moderately high can ships or even lifeboats pass in or out — and it inevitably takes time.

25. If the canal could not be used, the only means of getting the lifeboat into the sea was to take her across the canal by the swing-bridge, round the Crescent and along the Strand whence the sands of Summerleaze Beach and the sea were accessible, whatever the state of the tide. Even this took time. This photograph, taken about 1910, shows the launching-carriage with *Elizabeth Moore Garden II* being towed along the Strand by a team of horses, led by the town band and escorted by police and a small crowd. The crew rides in state with oars aloft. The ceremony suggests that no ketch was breaking up on the rocks or floundering in the bay but that a demonstration was being given.

26. This photograph shows the lifeboat going to the rescue of the ketch *Alford* in 1908. The team of horses had to take the launching-carriage into water deep enough for the boat to float – stern first to avoid damage to the rudder. Once afloat, the crew took over with their oars. Fortunately the lifeboat was not the only means of saving life. First a 'Life Mortar', then a rocket with breeches-buoy apparatus were installed at Bude and housed in the little building, now a dwelling, near the end of Breakwater Road. As soon as a line had been shot across a rock-bound or stranded vessel, there was a link with the land; crew members could be brought ashore or a rescue party put on board.

27. This photograph shows the lifeboat crew of 1924, the last to serve before the boat was withdrawn because of the small amount of shipping using the harbour and the improved margin of safety resulting from auxiliary engines. The names, from left to right, are (standing): G. Rowe, Coxswain Harry Barrett, G. Darch, G. Johnson, C. Thorn, G. Abbott, H. Marshall and H. Bate; (seated): H. Batten (partly obscured), G. Sangwin, A. Jewell, G. Marshall and H. Stapleton. The boat is in the canal; the crew-men, all volunteers, are correctly dressed in their cork life-jackets the absence of which had once cost Coxswain Maynard his life (see no. 17). These men are the predecessors of those who man the rescue services today.

Summerlease Beach Bude

11558

28. This photograph of Summerleaze Beach from the edge of the down was taken about 1925. Beach Tea Rooms had replaced the earlier Coronation Tea Rooms, but Munster Cottage and Penrock had not been built, nor had the concrete wall where the nearest row of tents stands in this picture. There was no car park, and the dunes were quite extensive. The tents and mobile huts did little damage to the natural environment. Most of the dunes have now gone — though welcome attempts are being made to protect what is left — and the beach is more stony than it used to be. Efford Down House still privately owned, the Rocket House and Breakwater Road cottages can be seen beyond the canal; and there are more trees than we find today. The Castle (see no. 51) is in the top left hand corner of the picture.

29. Now known as Crooklets, Maer Ladies Bathing Beach had been used exclusively by ladies from an early date — to avoid the prying eyes of seamen, no doubt, though the sexes were segregated at many resorts. Facilities were provided by the Morris and Penfound families. This photograph (from 1904) shows the beach in its unaltered condition. It is now backed by a sea-wall and equipped with permanent bathing cabins and other facilities including the important and most necessary headquarters of that admirable organization Bude Surf Life Saving Club. One result of these developments, which have disturbed the natural flow of sand, is that there are more stones on the beach.

47130. BUDE: MAER LAKE BATHING BEACH.

30. This photograph covers part of the same ground as no. 29 but was taken some ten years later looking back across the area now built over or occupied by a large car park. The beach was no longer reserved for ladies only. Mixed bathing has at last been accepted, though the clothing of both sexes seems totally incongruous for a summer day on the beach. You might say the same, however, of the near nakedness of today when a cold wind is blowing off the sea. In the background are six substantial private residences one of which is now Penarvor Hotel, formerly the home of Sir George Croydon Marks, Liberal M.P. for North Cornwall. These buildings have remained relatively unchanged in appearance; the main developments in this area have been just outside this view.

31. Until the coming of the railway in 1898, the horse-drawn coach was the main land-link between Bude, Stratton and the rest of England. There were at least four operators in the town – Brendon, Cobbledick, Pridham and Blatchford – and they gave good service in most directions: to Okehampton and Exeter, Barnstaple, Boscastle, Tintagel, Launceston and Plymouth. And the coaches bore brave names such as 'Defiance' and 'Flying Dutchman'. This photograph, which was taken after 1894 when the parish hall (visible in the background) was built, shows coaches outside the old post office and Bray's chemist and stationary business-sites now occupied by the National Westminster Bank and Boots. Also visible are the Norfolk Hotel which has recently closed, and the old Blanchminster boarding house, now Barclay's Bank.

32. This photograph of coaches outside the Falcon Hotel must have been taken at about the same time as the last one. The stage coach called at the Falcon as well as the post office, and would go straight to Efford Down House before making any official stops if Arthur Mills had anyone coming to stay; this was the regular custom, so we have been told. There were those who thought that the railway spoilt the last miles of the journey to Bude as there was a real thrill about the coach drive with the first smell of the sea and the first sight of the Storm Tower from the high ground on the Holsworthy side of Stratton. You can still get the same view from your car, but not the same smell, if you aren't in too much of a hurry.

33. As soon as the London and South Western Railway reached Holsworthy in 1888, a local committee (Holsworthy and Bude Railway Company) was formed, and two years later the first sod was cut by the wife of Canon Thynne of Kilkhampton. The original date for completion of the scheme was October 1891. But there were complications. The route was altered, and Stratton lost its promised station. It was August 1898 before the job was done. Directors arrived from Exeter in a special train and drove in open carriages through triumphal arches in the town – 'Progress' and 'Success Railway' notices appeared. A banquet was held, toasts were given and Bude Band played. *Most Beautiful Bude, the Gem of the West/ Thy lovely surroundings all make for the Best.*

34. Bude was a terminus of what became in 1923 the Southern Railway. It boasted a bookstall, a goods station and even a shunting yard in which this engine and the station staff were photographed in 1905. You could reach Bude from Waterloo without changing. There were Bude carriages in the front of the train at the end of the long platform. A fine main-line engine took you to Exeter. You were then shunted on to a side-line and proceeded ever more slowly to Okehampton, Halwill Junction where more carriages were dropped, and eventually Bude. If you were lucky enough to secure a corner seat the journey could be extraordinarily pleasant. It was a sad day when the railway was cut off less than seventy years after the opening banquet. Bungalows now adorn the station site.

35. This view of Stratton, taken in 1913 from Howell's Bridge, now the main road bridge, shows how the little market town clusters round the ancient church of St. Andrew – 'tall Stratton tower' watching over the community is how the Reverend R.S. Hawker described it. Owing to its position on a hill-top the church is difficult to see entire. Parts of it date from the 14th century when the crusader Sir Ranulph Blanchminster expressed a wish to be buried in the aisle. His effigy is preserved in the church; there is also a fine brass (1561) of Sir John Arundell and his two wives. Both these families had owned the manor of Efford, which included much of modern Bude, in ancient times.

36. This much earlier photograph of Stratton was taken in the 1880s; again the tall church tower forms the background. The couple in the foreground are Mr. and Mrs. Dell about whom nothing seems now to be known. They are standing in front of a group of buildings which include The New Inn. It seems to have been unoccupied, and the exposed hearth suggests that some demolition had already taken place. The rest of these buildings were cleared away shortly afterwards, the space being given the name of Jubilee Square in 1887. Stratton's St. Andrew's Fair was customarily held on this site.

Alexandra Oil

62399

37. This photograph, looking down Fore Street, Stratton, shows the entrance to The Tree Inn and, on the left, an old building now demolished. It was taken before 1914 as the cart-track in the road is clearly visible. The Tree Inn, now a well appointed hostelry, had been the local manor house — not occupied by the lord but by his factor or some other retainer. Best known among them was the 17th century giant, Anthony Payne, who served the Grenvilles during the Civil War and attended upon the gallant Sir Bevil at the Battle of Stamford Hill (in Stratton) in May 1643. Stratton was the seat of justice for a wide area — the Stratton magistrates still function but their bench now sits in Bude. Both Leet and Baron Courts were held annually in The Tree Inn until the 1900s.

38. This picture of a party of Stratton children setting off on their annual Sunday School outing was taken in 1914. It is very typical of the sort of excursion that was arranged for children at this and in earlier times. George Sangwin is holding the leading horse with Canon Leslie Jones, vicar of Stratton, alongside the waggon – he does not seem to be accompanying his flock. There still are Sangwins in the area. The daughter of Canon Jones married Spencer Howlett, a well-known Bude resident, sometime chairman of the local branch of the Old Cornwall Society and a Cornish bard.

39. This picture of a donkey and trap, carrying two unnamed ladies, was taken about 1912 in a part of Stratton known as Sanctuary — donkeys were not used extensively in this way though this animal seems ready enough for its task. Before the Reformation, this area was part of the Manor of Sanctuary held by the Augustinian monks of Launceston Priory. At the dissolution of the monasteries in the 16th century most of the manor was annexed to the Duchy of Cornwall. An interesting result of this is that Prince Charles, Duke of Cornwall, remains to this day patron of the living of St. Andrew's Church, Stratton.

40. It is probable that this photograph of a group of Stratton worthies, craftsmen and traders, was taken in 1887 – they are natural successors to the 'Eight Men of Stratton' who managed the affairs of the town in mediaeval and Tudor times. They are outside The New Inn (see no. 36) which is plastered with notices each one of which tells its own story. From left to right the worthies are: (back row) William Pickard, farmer and agent of the Grenville estate; William Rathenbury, watchmaker; Nicholas Saunders, cordwainer (shoemaker) and superintendant registrar; William Maynard, carpenter; William Yeo, cordwainer; J.R. Edgcombe, ironmonger, plumber and master of a scratch pack of foxhounds; (front row) Thomas Woodley, blacksmith later grocer; William Moyse, barber and precentor of the Wesleyan chapel; Peter Bray, auctioneer and printer; John Hearn, labourer; and James Peardon who had served at Waterloo as a drummer boy.

41. This picture, taken in 1886 or 1887, shows Nicholas Saunders (born 1822 and one of the worthies in the last photograph) surrounded by some of his children, grandchildren and workmen. They are (from left to right): Bert Saunders, Alfred Saunders, Lydia Saunders and her children (Madge, Frank and Ethel), Ellen Brown, Charles Saunders, Fanny Lark and Mary Jane, the wife of Nicholas. By the workshops are Bill Penfound, Robert Govier and John Hoare with Charles Yeo on the steps. The boot and shoe shop was part of Marshall's Cottage. The workshop was converted into Lilac Cottage in 1903 and still stands. The business flourished. Saunders Footwear Limited now has branches in Newquay, Padstow, Wadebridge, Perranporth, Holsworthy and Bude. But there is no longer a shop in Stratton.

42. This is another interesting group of Stratton folk, dating from the same period, and was taken near Howell's Bridge. The King's Arms Hotel, which still serves the public, is just visible in the background. Nicholas Treleaven, wheelwright, is on the right in front of his premises. Reuben Cory, wearing a leather apron, stands before the door while the more distant figure is William Moyse, barber, known by the unusual nickname of 'Lady Harriett'. The vehicle on the left is a typical Cornish wain, universally used for bringing in the harvests whether of corn or hay. *Tools were made and born were hands,/ As every farmer understands.* (William Blake.)

43. These school children were photographed early in the present century, standing beside the River Neet in Stratton. The buildings were known as Leat Cottages, a name which derived from the leat which served Howard's Mill and possibly also the old tannery, seen in the background but long since demolished. Tanning was once a thriving business, based on the bark of oak trees from woods in the area; bark was also exported to Ireland by sea. Some of these old oak woods still stand but in the largest of them, the Swannacott Woods near Week St. Mary, most of the oaks have been uprooted to make room for alien conifers — an unfortunate but probably necessary change in commercial terms.

44. The blizzard of 1891, when this photograph was taken, has passed into the folklore of the West but may have been no worse than that of 1978. One story has already been told (see no. 18). *Ceres* fared better than *Ant*. She was caught in the great gale when sailing from Padstow to Plymouth with a cargo of slates but rounded Land's End safely. The little ketch *Francis Beddoe*, which often visited the haven, was carrying slate from Gloucester to Bideford but was blown right down the coast to St. Ives; the only crew member still functioning was her master, Captain Slade. The damage inland does not seem to have been recorded but there was plenty of snow for these people to clear up at the bottom of Landsdown Road, opposite the old 'water shute'.

45. This photograph shows the top of Belle Vue, now Bude's main shopping street, at the beginning of the 1880s. The left hand building was Springfield Cottage, one section of which was the home of Monty Thorn, carriage proprietor. The thatched house was occupied by a butcher named Tucker while the slated building stood at the end of Othello Terrace, a development which preceded the canal. When the terrace was demolished, some years after this photograph was taken, Dr. Arthur King built Grosvenor House on the site; and this, in turn, has become shops with flats above. There were many developments in this neighbourhood before 1930 including the premises of Spencer Thorn and N.T. Keat, both established before the end of the last century, and the main post office which opened in 1924.

46. This photograph of the Strand was taken in 1882 from roughly the position now occupied by Lloyds Bank. Immediately opposite is the original Globe Hotel where on 25th August 1886, Roy Thorn's grandmother booked in two holiday-makers for one night and breakfast, thereby inaugurating the 'bed and breakfast' business. The adjoining buildings, then known as Tapson's Terrace, were described as 'lodging houses for the quality'. Further along the road was Angove House, occupied by a general merchant called Avery, and the premises of Gurney and Craven, solicitors. Angove House, now a shopping arcade called Julia's Place, has also been Sam Edwards' garage and a bus centre. The Carrier's Inn, originally a farm, was being run by the Cobbledick family when this photograph was taken. Beyond it are warehouses.

47. This is a later picture of the Strand, taken in 1914, when it was beginning to look much more modern with the reconstructed Globe Hotel, Medland's (ladies' outfitter) and Lovell's (wine merchant) both with sun-blinds as well as Gurney and Craven, solicitors who also serviced the urban district council. In the centre of the picture you can see Granville Tea Rooms, formerly the old Bude Hotel, on the site where Lloyds Bank was established in 1923. The Grenville Hotel had recently been opened, its bulk somewhat incompatible in scale with other buildings in Bude. The Summerleaze Crescent houses stand out along the skyline.

Blanchminster Square

48. The name Blanchminster Square has vanished from the map of Bude to be replaced by Shute Triangle. The change is unfortunate. The old name has a very ancient link with the area (see no. 35) and is commemorated by the Blanchminster Charity which was founded in the 15th century and which still functions distributing funds to the needy, providing educational grants and doing other good works. The Charity owns property in this neighbourhood and in Lansdown Road up which the motor-cyclist in this picture is proceeding. A turning off Lansdown Road leads to King Street, built in the 1840s on a site formerly known as Popy's Place – another property of the Charity. This photograph, taken in 1921, shows the Central Methodist Church complex and the Drill Hall, originally a chapel. Wonnacott's Dairy (see no. 58) is at the extreme left.

49. This photograph gives a remarkably good impression of Bude as it was in 1904. On the left is Belmont House, now the International Stores, and then the houses, business premises and shops on the east side of Belle Vue which must then have deserved its name; in the distance are the King Street houses, then known as Tiger Bay, where many local seafaring men once lived. Some of the central group of buildings still stand but the houses known as Marine Terrace have been demolished. Beyond are the Strand buildings with, across the bridge, the Methodist church and the saltings of the River Neet now occupied by tennis courts, bowling green and squash courts. Much of the open ground is now dominated by the Grenville Hotel.

Bude Harbour from Granville Terrace

50. The Old Bude Bridge is better known as Nanny Moore's after a well-known 19th century 'dipper' who lived in the cottage. Leven Cottage is of considerable antiquity, and one wall includes a granite block inscribed 'AJA 1589' for 'Anne and John Arundell'. It was originally Efford Mill which was worked by the run of the tide. The cottage was Cobbledick's bakery when this photograph was taken about 1910; it then became Ash's and, during the 1930s, Parsons Brothers so that continuity with the past and with the milling and baking trades is unbroken. The Castle, Storm Tower and the cottages which overlook the harbour can be seen in the background as well as the breakwater and ships waiting for the tide.

51. This photograph of croquet on The Castle lawn was taken about 1890. The house, which is now owned and used as offices by the local authority, was built by the eminent Victorian engineer and inventor, Sir Goldsworthy Gurney, who designed a 'steam coach' which ran from London to Bath and back before the coming of the railways. The Castle, Gurney's first Cornish home, was erected on a sand-dune site leased from Sir Thomas Acland in the 1830s. It remained in private hands until the Second World War. The Castle occupies a very central position in Bude; it provides not only offices but a seat for the Stratton magistrates and accommodation for the local branch of the county library. Numerous public functions take place in the grounds.

52. The church of St. Michael and All Angels, Bude Haven, was built by Sir Thomas Acland in 1835 as a chapel-of-ease served from Stratton, becoming an independent parish church twelve years later. Though basically simple in structure it was extended on more than one occasion and refurbished to provide an essentially satisfying interior. Among vicars during the fifty years between 1880 and 1930 were the Reverend Barton Mills, grandson of the church's founder, and Doctor Edmund Burr, who revived the ancient ceremony of 'blessing the sea'. In 1921, the advowson was given to the Diocesan Board so assuring that the people of the parish would have a proper say in the appointment of their vicar. This is by no means always the case.

45935. BUDE: EFFORD COTTAGE & CHAPEL ROCK.

53. Efford Cottage, which lies just outside the sea-lock, was built by Sir Thomas Acland in the 1820s on the site of an old cottage where fishermen used to salt their fish; this was incorporated into the building. At the same time he built the two cottages next door. Hereabouts there was also an old lime kiln all traces of which have disappeared. Used mainly as a summer residence by relatives and friends of the owners, Efford Cottage remained in the Acland family until the 1940s. It was very little changed during those years though a garage, unobtrusively cut into the hillside, was added during the 1920s. For a time it was known locally as Ivy Cottage.

54. Ebbingford, once a manor house of the Arundells of Trerice, was given to the parish of Bude Haven by Sir Thomas Acland to serve as a vicarage — it was a vicarage when this photograph was taken in the early 1900s. It was sold in the 1950s when the vicar moved to Falcon Terrace, less imposing but more practical. Ebbingford then became the home of the late Sir Dudley Stamp, the geographer. The house has a long history. In 1413 it was licensed as an oratory so that mass could be said in the domestic chapel. And in May 1643, on the eve of the Battle of Stamford Hill in which they were victorious, the commanders of the Royalist Cornish Army held there a 'councell of warr'.

55. This photograph, taken from below the Summerleaze cliffs in the 1880s, shows Efford Cottage with a much lower sea-wall than we see today, the sea-lock, East and West Cottages and the imposing Efford Down House in the background. The latter, built in 1848, was the home of Arthur Mills, M.P. for Exeter in the 1880s and for many years a leading figure in the Bude community. Following the death of his son, Barton the former vicar, in 1932 Efford Down became a hotel; enlargement and alterations did not change the character of the building. East and West Cottages were used at different times as additional accommodation for Efford Cottage, by Efford Down staff and by coastguards before becoming private homes in the 1890s. The first building to be put up beside the road to the left of East Cottage was the Rocket House; other houses followed in the 1920s.

56. This photograph of the staff of Messrs Hockin, Banbury & Company, agricultural and general merchants, was probably taken shortly before 1923 when the business was taken over by J.W. Fulford & Sons of Bideford. In the centre of the group is the chairman, Mr. G.W.W. Banbury, who was also Lloyds agent in the area; his sons, Garfield and Ralph, sit on either side of him. Both office and yard staff are included in the group. The business had been set up in Bude by John Hockin early in the 19th century and was continued by him in partnership with Henry Hooper. In 1881 J.W. Banbury came in first as managing director and later as partner. The business expanded and diversified to include coal, wool buying and eventually timber and other requirements of the building trade.

57. Taken at the Stratton Agricultural Show in 1927 or 1928, this photograph shows George Brendon and Alfred Petherick admiring a fine bull. At this period the Brendon family (former holders of the Poughill manor) owned the Falcon Hotel and leased Efford Farm; George Brendon himself had continued to operate a horse-drawn coach service until 1910 – believed to be last such service in the country. Alfred Petherick was head of the long established and still active family firm of corn and coal merchants with wharehouses on the wharfs and coastal vessels including *Ceres*. He was for some years an active chairman of Bude-Stratton Urban District Council.

58. Annie Heard is seen driving Wonnacott's milk-cart along Vicarage Road in about 1916. The smart trotting pony, the polished urns from which milk was delivered straight into customers' own jugs, and the butter-yellow cart with black lettering were familiar sights. And the service was as immaculate as the equipment. Wonnacotts still farm at Rodd's Bridge, alongside the first lock on the upper canal, but are no longer active dairymen. The mixed farm helps to supply their thriving 'wholefood' and fresh produce business near the top of Lansdown Road; the older shop at the other end of the same road, where the dairy was situated in the early years of this century (see no. 48), was closed in 1984.

Opening of the New Sewerage Works at Bude 1st Aug 1909

S. Thorn Photo Bude

59. The opening of a public sewer may seem a strange subject for a picture postcard but this one was popular locally when it was produced in 1909. And those of us who are old enough to remember those dreadful earth closets in the garden can see the point. The new system which pumped, and still pumps, untreated sewage into the sea is now in the process of being replaced. The ceremony was held at a trap-door on the Efford Downs with the Storm Tower in the background. The door allows access to the beach and outflow system by means of a long ladder and a mysterious spiral staircase which winds down into the bowels of the earth. No one now knows who officiated. It was not General Sir Redvers Buller as is commonly supposed, though he had opened a new water-supply a few years earlier.

60. Fairs have been part of the English tradition for centuries, the Stratton fair being first allowed by a charter of King John in 1207. As Bude grew in the 19th century, the fairs were switched away from Stratton (see no. 36), one being held at Whitsuntide and another at Michaelmas. But the first thing that strikes you about this picture of Fair Day at Bude in 1910 is that parking problems are not new. The Strand is filled with all manner of horse-drawn vehicles. This photograph also shows a stage in that street's development slightly earlier than no. 47. The two hard-hatted worthies in the foreground are Job Hockaday, retired manager of Delabole slate quarry who lived to be a centenarian and Bude's oldest inhabitant, and Samuel Banbury, farmer and stock-breeder.

61. Bude Band was established in 1883 as part of a unit of volunteers attached to the Duke of Cornwall's Light Infantry. This photograph was taken some fifteen or twenty years later in front of the Seamen's Mission which eventually became headquarters of the Bude Boy Scouts – the band, entirely independent of the DCLI, now has its own Band Hall beside the canal. The bandmaster in this photograph was Mr. Hancock, a local tailor, and he can be seen with his baton sitting immediately to the left of the big drum. Not all the bandsmen can be identified but they include (standing) E. Legg and G. Lock, among the clarinet players, C. Thorn with his cornet, third from the right, (sitting) Mr. Yeo and Mr. Cann with, extreme right, George Abbot.

Coronation Day, Bude.
Church Parade. 22-6-1911. Beach Hill.

62. The coronation of King George V in 1911 was widely celebrated with parades, church services, banquets and bonfires. In this photograph the Bude Band is seen leading a unit of the Volunteers across the swing-bridge towards St. Michael's Church. Prominent in the background are (far right) Rosevear Villas, now flats, and Bencoolen House, now a licensed restaurant. The house was named after the barque *Bencoolen* which was wrecked in 1863 with the loss of twenty-four lives. It was built by Oliver Davey, merchant and owner of the schooner *Annie Davey* (see no. 17), who is believed to have included in the roof timbers from the wrecked barque. An old stable at the back of the building was once part of Call's Farm.

Bude. Unveiling of War Memorial Nov 22.

63. This postcard shows the Bude War Memorial being unveiled on 11th November 1922, with a guard-of-honour of local Territorials, the vicar (Dr. Burr) and a large crowd most of whom would have had relatives or friends among the 64 names on the monument which is topped by the torch emblem of Talbot House, better known as Toc H. The names of 38 Second World War victims were added later. The site is at the top of Shaldern Hill and lies between the Crescent and the Central Methodist Church. The memorial has been the centre of every subsequent Armistice or Remembrance Day parade as have similar monuments throughout Britain. Stratton and most of the surrounding villages have their own War Memorials.

64. This photograph of the cottage just above the beach at Northcott Mouth was taken just before the 1880s but is typical of many rural dwellings in the area until at least the first decade of the present century. There still is only one cottage on the site, but it is not easy to say how much if any of the old building has been retained. Outside the cottage are John and Mary Curtis who were succeeded by two generations of the Brock family. These people worked on the land and may have fished occasionally, though there are no signs of nets or lobster pots. They would certainly have collected edible seaweeds and wood from the beach; and flotsam from the sea must have provided useful pickings as the rocky coast a few yards from the cottage was a dangerous area for shipping.

MARHAMCHURCH

65. This photograph of the old smithy at Marhamchurch was taken about 1920 when the local blacksmith and his forge were still prominent in every village in the land. This small smithy and the thatched cottage beside it were demolished in 1926 when the last Marhamchurch blacksmith, S. Jeffrey, ceased to ply his trade. Very few true farrier's smithies now remain. One which does is the Old Forge on the wharf at Bude (see no. 12) but no farrier works in the building which is now the town museum. Although the forge is carefully preserved, the fire is represented by a light, and the various hammers, tongs and other tools are silent.

66. The church of St. Morwenna at Marhamchurch, with the War Memorial in the open space in front of it, was photographed in 1921. The church is old and includes some Norman masonry; the tower is low but well proportioned and makes an appropriate centre to the village. As are several other churches in the neighbourhood, it is decorated by the Royal Arms granted by King Charles II to certain parishes which had been loyal to his father and the Royalist cause during the Civil War. The most remarkable feature of the church, however, is a niche which leads from the aisle to an anchorite's cell built in 1404 for Cecilia Mays.

67. This photograph, taken in 1911, of Week St. Mary — once a borough in name but no more than a village in size — shows well the tall unbuttressed tower of 'Our Lady of Week' and a typical village shop and post office of the period. The place owes the tower to its most famous inhabitant, Thomasine Bonaventura, a young shepherd girl who guarded sheep on the commons during the 15th century. Thomasine was taken to London by a visiting wool merchant who later married her. She was twice widowed and eventually became the wife of Sir John Percyval who was elected Lord Mayor of London the following year, 1498. Soon widowed yet again and now a considerable heiress, she returned to Week and carried out many good works including the church tower and, just beyond the limits of this photograph, a foundation known as Old College, parts of which still exist in good condition thanks to careful restoration by the Landmark Trust.

Launcells,
Nr Bude. (2)

68. This photograph of Launcells might have been taken at almost any time during the past hundred years but actually dates from 1930. It shows the church of St. Andrew, the fine old barton with its farm buildings and a countryside which is still farmed with a decent respect for tradition. It is and always has been a beautiful peaceful place with mature trees as well as ancient buildings and a mediaeval holy well, dedicated to St. Swithin, near the church. The church itself has beautyful carved bench-ends and 15th century tiles on the chancel floor where heraldic lions, Tudor roses and the pelican of Christian mythology can be identified.

POUGHILL VILLAGE, BUDE

69. Poughill has always been a well kept village but seems to have lacked many of the amenities which gave most villages their particular characteristics — there was no inn before the 1980s. Old buildings, including these former almshouses, have changed little but several substantial Victorian and Edwardian houses were built well back from the road, while more recent housing estates have been kept out of sight. The church is of great interest and bears an unusual dedication to St. Olaf; the lych-gate, just visible in this 1920s photograph, was built in 1897. There are bench-ends like those at Launcells, the Royal Arms and a tablet commemorating the life of Sir Goldsworthy Gurney (see no. 51) which reminds us that he had brought about the adoption of a standard time throughout England — until the middle of the 19th century even Exeter used its own time.

Rev. R.S. Hawker Late Vicar
Moorwenstow. (Photo ... Bude

70. We have included this picture of the Reverend
Robert Stephen Hawker, who died just before 1880,
as being the most representative Victorian character in
this part of Cornwall. Born at Stratton, married to a
daughter of Ebbingford (see no. 54) and idiosyncratic
vicar of Morwenstow for most of his working life, his
name and memory are still with us. Author and poet,
he has been the subject of both legends and books, the
best of which is *Hawker of Morwenstow* by Piers
Brendon, scion of an old Bude family (see no. 57).
Hawker wrote poems of pity for the many tragedies of
the sea and of anger when he reckoned, often wrongly,
that the rescue services were failing in their duty: *Ho!
Gossip for Bude Haven... the crew and skipper are
wallowing in the sea.*

Morwenstow Vicarage   *Thorn photo.*

71. Hawker's vicarage at Morwenstow, photographed in 1900, is undoubtedly the most remarkable Victorian building in the neighbourhood. There is nothing unusual about the house itself but the chimney-stacks must be unique; they were designed as replicas of towers of the churches with which Hawker had been associated: Stratton, Whitstone, North Tamerton and two Oxford towers. The kitchen chimney was copied from his mother's tomb. His ideal of the simple life is carved in stone above the door: *A house, a glebe, a pound a day/ A pleasant place to watch and pray;/ Be true to church, be kind to poor,/ O Minister for ever more.*

Widemouth.   Thorn photo

72. The Salt House at Widemouth Bay was virtually the only building in or near the bay when this photograph was taken, probably in 1912. The old road, which has now been eroded into the sea, is clearly identifiable as is Black Rock across the bay where the spirit of the evil Wrecker Featherstone is said to be imprisoned – his legendary task is to weave a rope of sand. Families used to walk across the cliffs from Bude in those days, spend a few hours catching prawns, which were then plentiful in pools on the Widemouth beach, eat a sumptuous cream tea outside the Salt House and return in a landau or Victoria hired from Edwards of Morwenna Terrace. The more robust walked both ways.

WIDEMOUTH BAY, Nr BUDE.

73. This photograph of Widemouth Bay, taken in the 1920s, shows an early stage in the unplanned, haphazard development which has not only changed but also disfigured this beautiful place. The photograph shows too the erosion of the low shale cliffs between the Salt House and the sea and, in the background, the pattern of fields enclosed by stonewall Cornish hedges. Fortunately the beaches and the sea, ideal for both children and surfers, cannot be changed. Individual houses occupy fine situations as do some of the small hotels – between them, these now cover much of the open ground in this picture – while many of the latter provide good fare and comfort.

Bude, Cornwall.　　P. 13705

74. This must be one of the first photographs of Bude from the air. Apparently taken in 1924, it shows Falcon Hotel in the bottom left-hand corner, the golf course in the middle distance — was the ladies' nine-hole course still functioning? — with Flexbury and some Poughill houses beyond, though not yet the building estates in those areas. Many features which are familiar today can be identified but the Recreation Ground is by no means complete. Coal is being delivered by rail to Petherick's yard on the lower wharf. There is hardly a car to be seen. The cottages of the Crescent, still well preserved, come out particularly well. They were built in the 1830s when the Crescent was called South Terrace or, for some reason unknown, Frying Pan Row. The square building beside the river used to belong to the Thorn family who took most of the early photographs in this neighbourhood and many of the postcards in this collection.

75. As we reach the end of this collection, it is well to remind ourselves that the prosperity and early development of Bude were based on the ketches which traded in and out of the haven. This photograph shows just such a vessel rounding Chapel Rock (see no. 4) as she leaves the harbour under full sail on an unusually calm day. We have not been able to identify this ketch with certainty but believe her to be *Clara May,* registered in Plymouth in the 1890s and brought to Bude by James Cornish in 1902. Bude remained her home port for twenty-one years; she then moved to Bideford. She had no engine while based on the haven but was so well maintained that she became known as Jimmy Cornish's yacht. She was finally laid up in 1953.

G36. LOW TIDE BUDE

76. This charming photograph of Summerleaze Beach at sunset, with the breakwater and Compass Point in the background, was taken by a relative of one of the authors and bought as a postcard in 1913 by the mother of the other. It shows the camera already in use as a form of artistic expression. It also makes an interesting comment on the change in public taste during the past seventy years to compare this picture with some of the garish colour reproductions that dominate most postcard racks today. But the scene remains the same. As John Betjeman says in 'Greenaway':

> *Tide after tide by night and day*
> *The breakers battle with the land*
> *And rounded smooth along the bay*
> *The faithful rocks protecting stand.*